LENNON & McCARTNEY
VOLUME 4

G000298751

HAL LEONARD® CORPORATION

7777 W. BLUEMOUND RD. P.O. BOX 13819 MILWAUKEE, WI 53213

Visit Hal Leonard Online at
www.halleonard.com

All My Loving

Words and Music by John Lennon and Paul McCartney

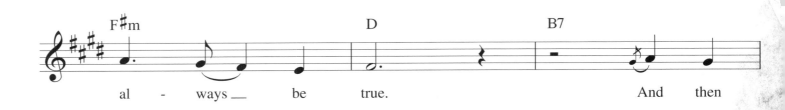

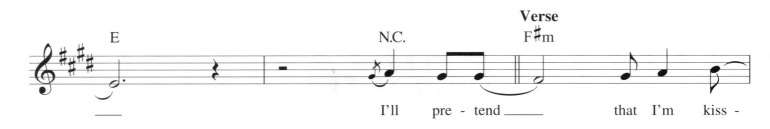

-ing the lips ____ I ____ am miss-ing and

hope that __ my dreams will __ come true.

And then while I'm a - way, ____ I'll write

home ev - 'ry day, _____ and I'll send all __ my

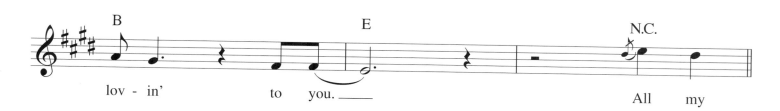

lov - in' to you. ____ All my

Chorus

Lead Vocal:

lov - in' I _____ will send to you. _____

Backing Vocals:

Ooh, _____

Interlude

Verse

All — my lov-in', dar-lin', I'll — be true. —

ooh. —

Close your eyes — and I'll kiss you. To-

Close your eyes — and I'll kiss you. To-

mor-row — I'll miss you. Re-mem-ber — I'll

mor-row — I'll miss you. Re-mem-ber — I'll

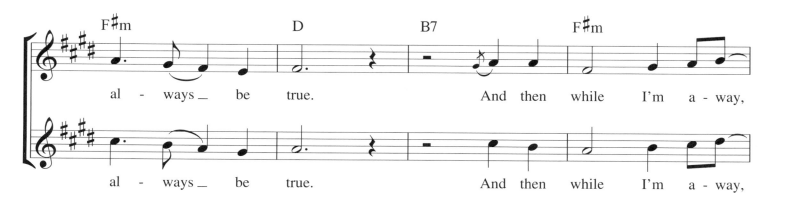

al - ways _ be true. And then while I'm a - way,

al - ways _ be true. And then while I'm a - way,

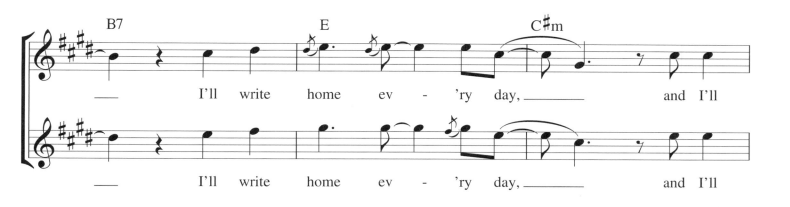

_ I'll write home ev - 'ry day, _____ and I'll

_ I'll write home ev - 'ry day, _____ and I'll

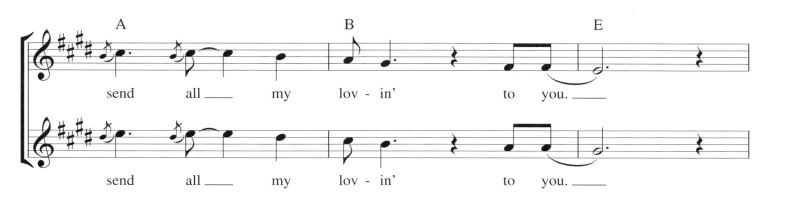

send all ___ my lov - in' to you. __

send all ___ my lov - in' to you. __

Chorus

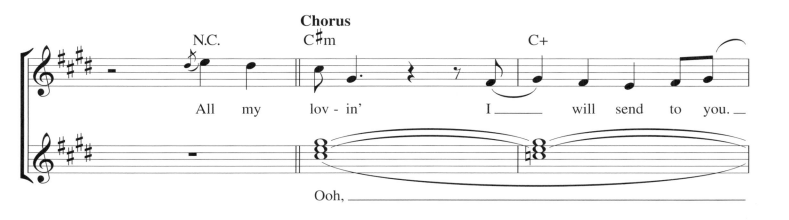

All my lov - in' I _____ will send to you. __

Ooh, _____

All ___ my lov - in', dar -

ooh. ___

Outro

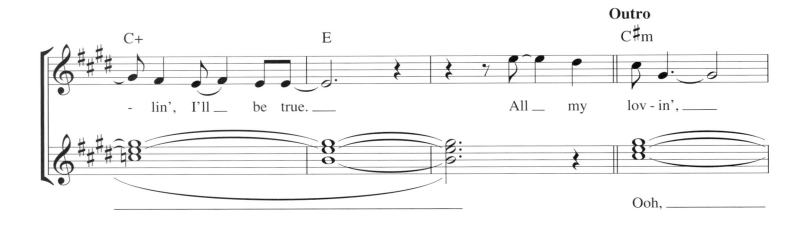

- lin', I'll ___ be true. ___ All ___ my lov - in', ___

Ooh, ___

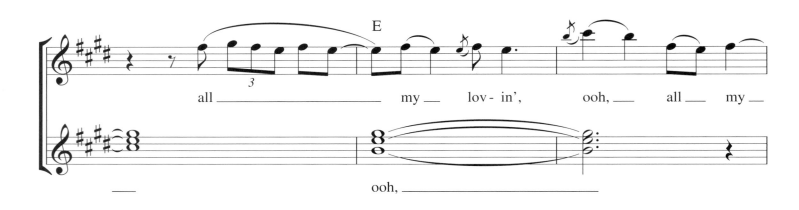

all ___ my ___ lov - in', ooh, ___ all ___ my ___

ooh, ___

___ lov - in' I will send to you.

ooh. ___

And I Love Her

Words and Music by John Lennon and Paul McCartney

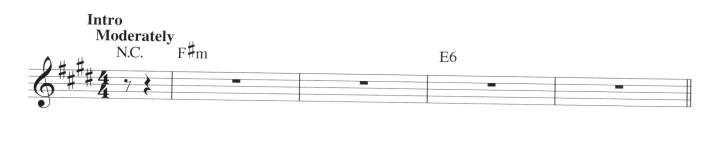

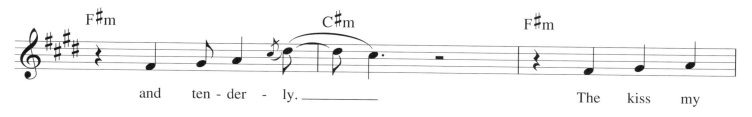

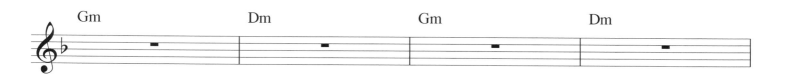

Verse

Bright are the stars ___ that shine, ___ dark is the sky. ___

___ I know this love of mine ___

will nev - er die, ___ and I love ___ her. ___

Outro

Day Tripper

Words and Music by John Lennon and Paul McCartney

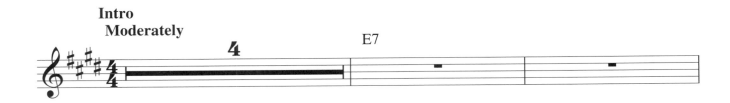

Verse

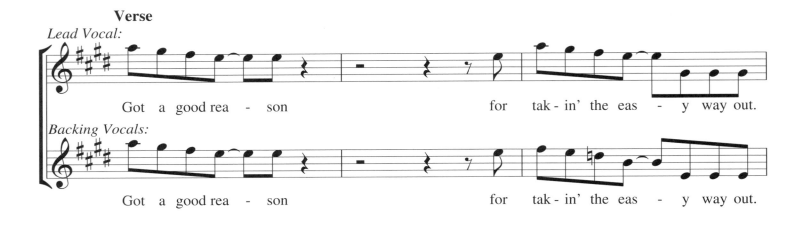

tak - in' the eas - y way out, ___ now. She was a day ___

tak - in' the eas - y way out, ___ now. She was a day

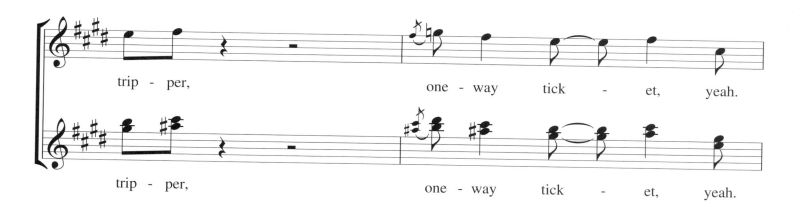

trip - per, one - way tick - et, yeah.

trip - per, one - way tick - et, yeah.

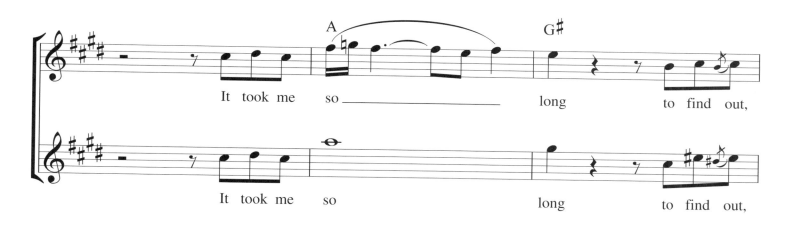

It took me so _____ long to find out,

It took me so long to find out,

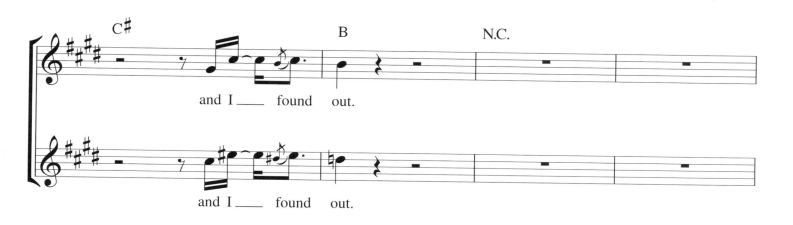

and I ___ found out.

and I ___ found out.

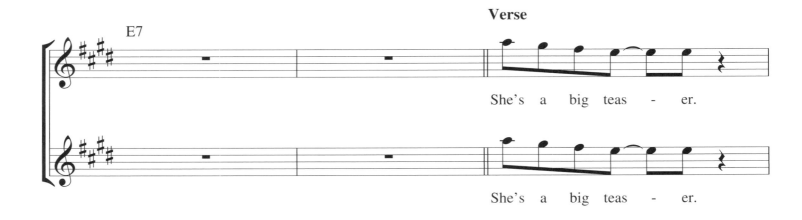

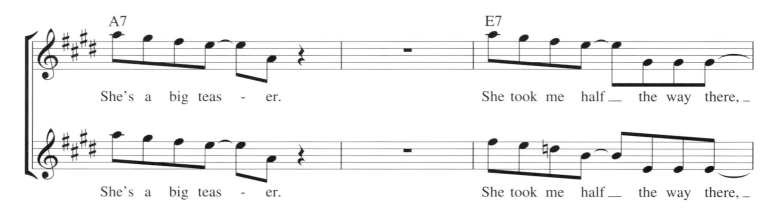

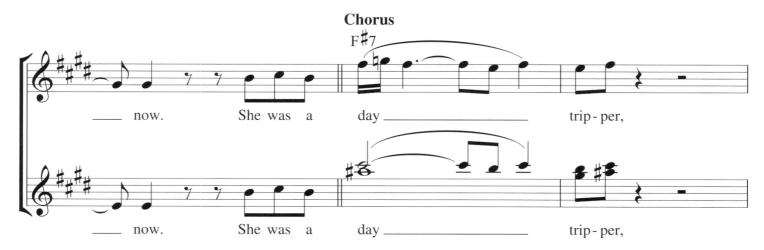

one-way tick - et, yeah.   It took me so _____

one-way tick - et, yeah.   It took me so

G#   C#   B

long   to find out,   and I ___ found   out.

long   to find out,   and I ___ found   out.

Bridge

Play 3 times

Ah, _____

Ah, _____

ah, _____   ah.

ah, _____   ah.

N.C.   E7

Verse

Lead Vocal:

Tried to please _ her. She on - ly played _ one - night stands. _

Backing Vocals:

Tried to please _ her. She on - ly played _ one - night stands. _

A7

_ Tried to please _ her.

_ Tried to please _ her.

E7   **Chorus**
                                                     F#7

She on - ly played _ one - night stands, _ now. She was a day _____

She on - ly played _ one - night stands, _ now. She was a day _____

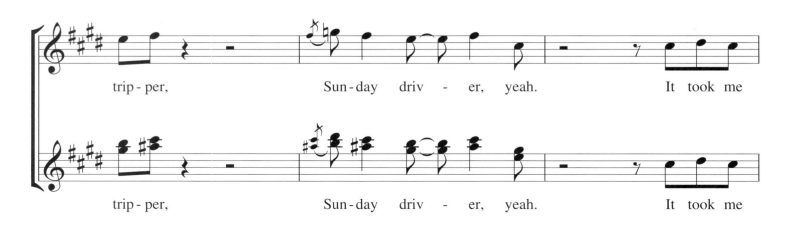

trip - per, Sun - day driv - er, yeah. It took me

trip - per, Sun - day driv - er, yeah. It took me

so _____ long   to find out,   and I ___ found

so   long   to find out,   and I ___ found

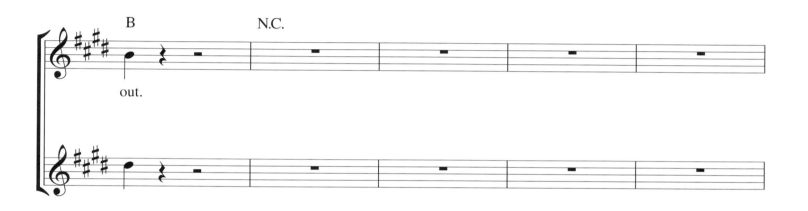

out.

Outro

Repeat and fade

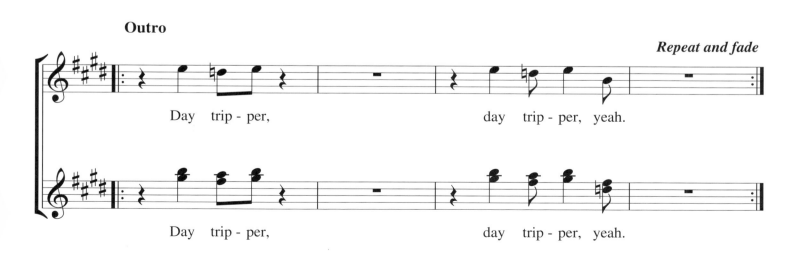

Day trip - per,   day trip - per, yeah.

Day trip - per,   day trip - per, yeah.

The Fool on the Hill

Words and Music by John Lennon and Paul McCartney

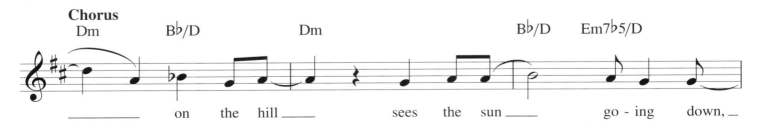

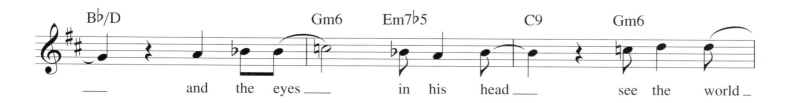

Bb/D   Gm6   Em7b5   C9   Gm6

___ and the eyes ___ in his head ___ see the world _

Dm   Dm6   Dm7   D6

___ spin - ning 'round. _____

Verse

D6

Well on the way,

G6/D   D6

head in a cloud, _____ the man of a thou - sand voic -

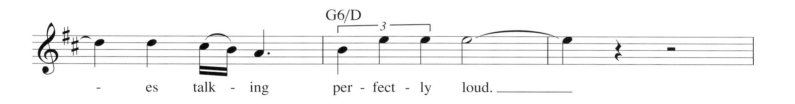

G6/D

- es talk - ing per - fect - ly loud. _____

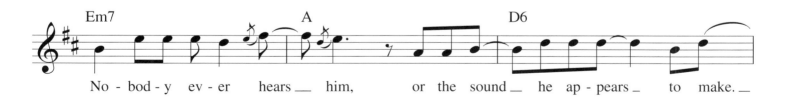

Em7   A   D6

No - bod - y ev - er hears ___ him, or the sound _ he ap - pears _ to make. _

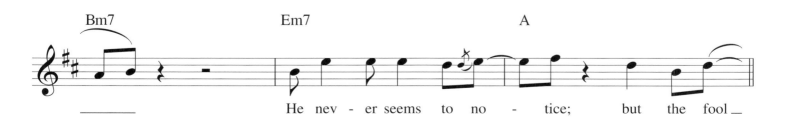

Bm7   Em7   A

_____ He nev - er seems to no - tice; but the fool _

Chorus

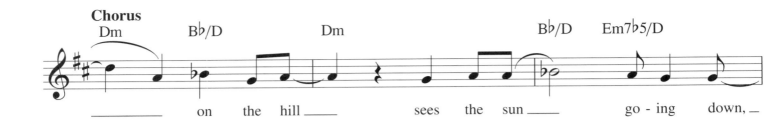

on the hill _____ sees the sun _____ go - ing down, _____

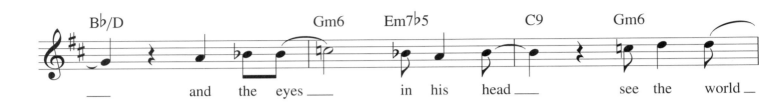

_____ and the eyes _____ in his head _____ see the world _____

_____ spin - ning 'round. _____

Interlude-Verse

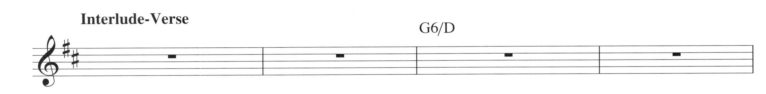

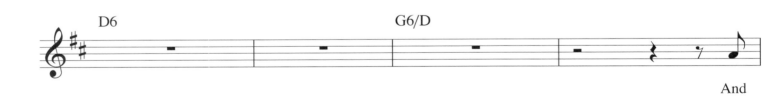

And

(Verse)

no - bod - y seems to like _____ him, they can tell _____ what he wants to do. _____

_____ He nev - er shows his feel - ings; but the fool _____

18

Em7   A   **Chorus** Dm   B♭/D

They don't ___ like him. The fool _____ on the hill

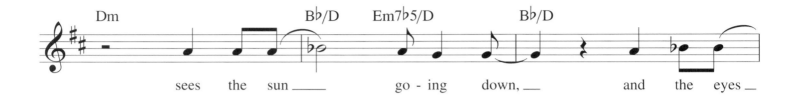

Dm   B♭/D   Em7♭5/D   B♭/D

sees the sun ___ go-ing down, ___ and the eyes ___

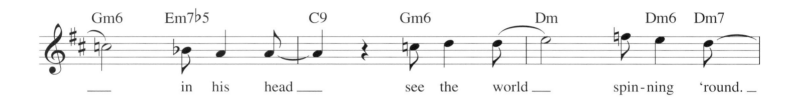

Gm6   Em7♭5   C9   Gm6   Dm   Dm6 Dm7

___ in his head ___ see the world ___ spin-ning 'round. ___

D6   **Outro** D6

___   Oh, _____

D6   G6/D

___ 'n' 'round, 'n' 'round, 'n' 'round.

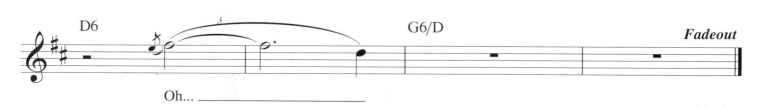

D6   G6/D   *Fadeout*

Oh... _____

I Saw Her Standing There

Words and Music by John Lennon and Paul McCartney

Intro
Brightly

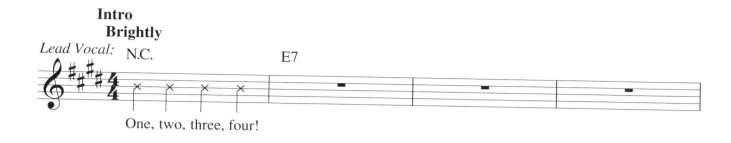

One, two, three, four!

Verse

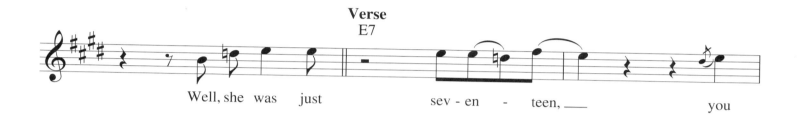

Well, she was just sev-en-teen, _____ you

know what I _____ mean, _____ and the way she looked was

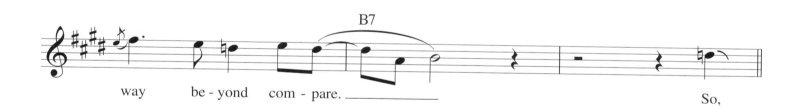

way be-yond com-pare. _____ So,

Chorus

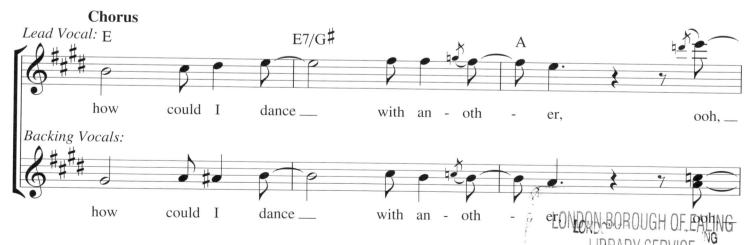

Lead Vocal: how could I dance _____ with an-oth-er, ooh, _____

Backing Vocals: how could I dance _____ with an-oth-er, ooh,

when I saw her stand - ing there. ___

when I saw her stand - ing there. ___

Verse

Lead Vocal:

Well, she ___ looked at ___ me, ___

and I, ___ I ___ could ___ see ___

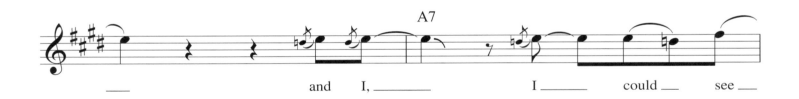

that be - fore too long I'd ___ fall in love _ with her. ___

Chorus

Lead Vocal:

___ She would - n't dance ___

Backing Vocals:

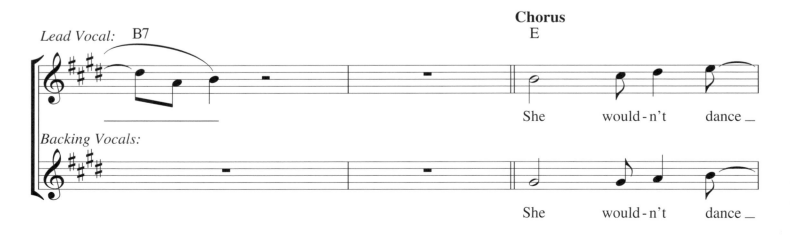

She would - n't dance ___

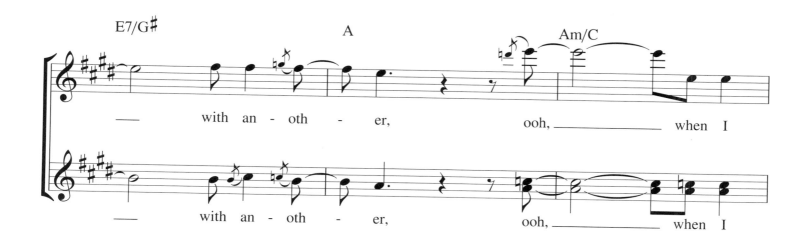

with an - oth - er, ooh, _____ when I

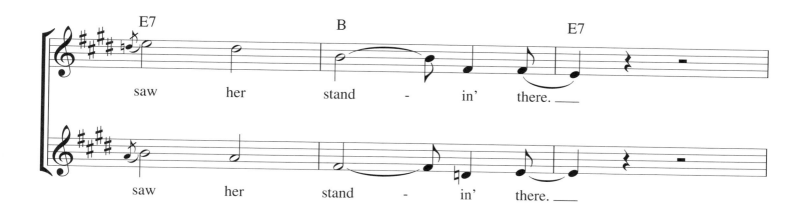

saw her stand - in' there. ___

Bridge

Well, my heart went boom __ when I

crossed that room, __ and I held her hand __

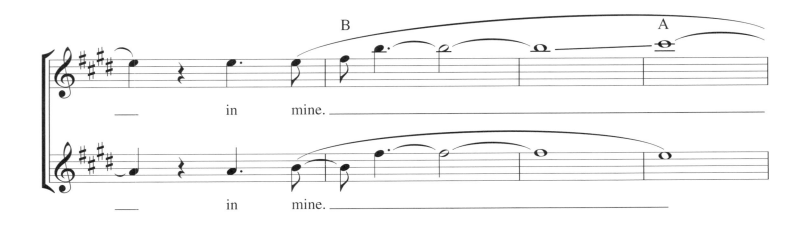

___ in mine.

___ in mine.

Lead Vocal:

%Verse

___ Oh, ___ we danced through the ___ night, ___ and we

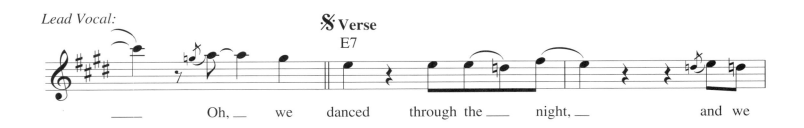

held each oth - er ___ tight, ___ and be - fore too long, I ___

___ fell in love ___ with her. ___ Now ___

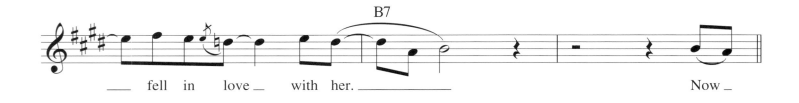

Chorus

Lead Vocal:

I'll nev - er dance ___ with an - oth - er, ooh, ___

Backing Vocals:

I'll nev - er dance ___ with an - oth - er, ooh, ___

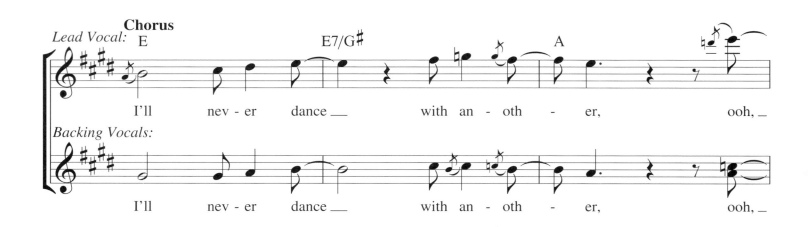

Am/C   E7   B   *To Coda* ⊕ E7

_____ since I saw her stand - in' there. _____ Wah! _____

_____ since I saw her stand - in' there. _____ Whoa!

Interlude

E7

B7   E7   E7/G♯

A   Am   E7   B7   E7

Bridge

Lead Vocal:

A

Well, my heart went boom _____ when I crossed that room, _

Backing Vocals:

Well, my heart went boom _____ when I crossed that room, _

25

D.S. al Coda

Coda

Outro

The Long and Winding Road

Words and Music by John Lennon and Paul McCartney

Verse
Moderate Ballad

Lead Vocal:

The long — and wind - ing road — that — leads —

— to your door — will nev - er dis - ap -

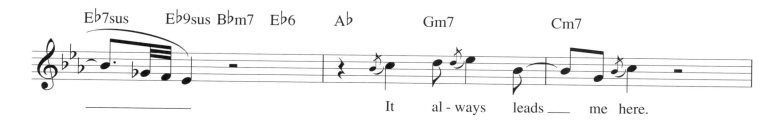

pear. I've seen that road — be - fore. —

It al - ways leads — me here.

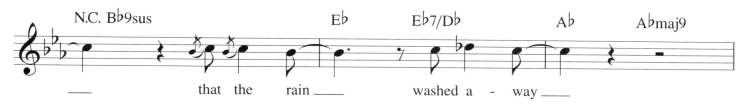

Lead me to your door. — The wild and wind - y night —

that the rain — washed a - way —

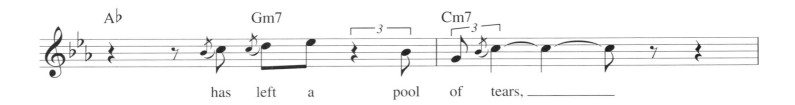

has left a pool of tears, _____

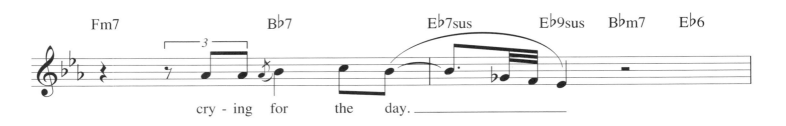

cry - ing for the day. _____

Why leave me stand - ing here?

Let me know _ the way. _____

Bridge

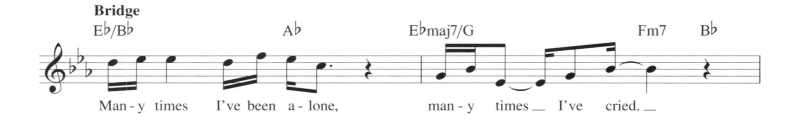

Man - y times I've been a - lone, man - y times _ I've cried. _

An - y - way, _____ you'll nev - er know the

Verse

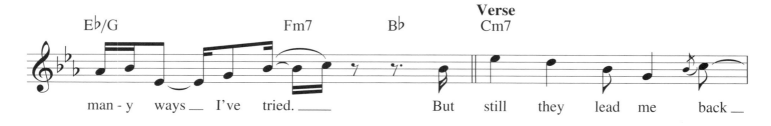

man - y ways _ I've tried. ____ But still they lead me back _

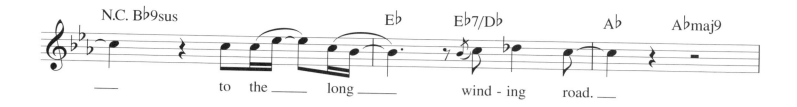

N.C. Bb9sus   Eb   Eb7/Db   Ab   Abmaj9

_____ to the _____ long _____ wind - ing road. _____

Ab   Gm7   Cm7

You left me stand - ing here

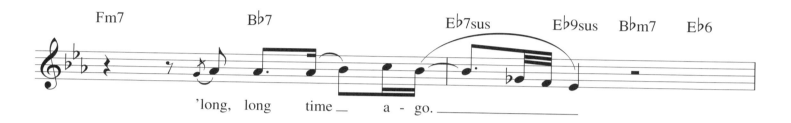

Fm7   Bb7   Eb7sus   Eb9sus   Bbm7   Eb6

'long, long time _____ a - go. _____

Ab   Gm7   Cm7

Don't keep me wait - ing here. _____

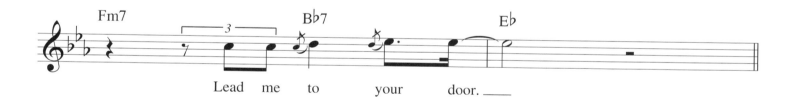

Fm7   3   Bb7   Eb

Lead me to your door. _____

Interlude

Eb/Bb   Ab6   Ebmaj7/G   Fm7   Bb9sus   Eb/Bb   Ab6

Verse

Ebmaj7/G   Fm7   Bb   Cm7

But still they lead me back _____

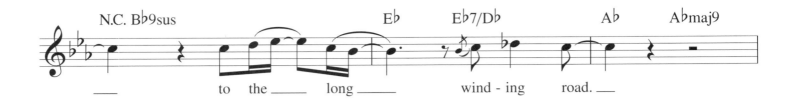

N.C. B♭9sus   E♭   E♭7/D♭   A♭   A♭maj9

to the ___ long ___ wind - ing road. ___

A♭   Gm7   3   Cm7

You left me stand - ing here

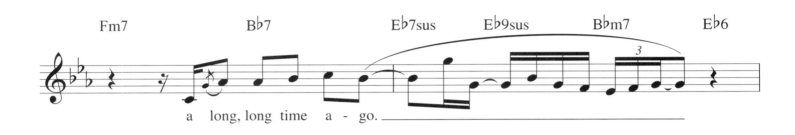

Fm7   B♭7   E♭7sus   E♭9sus   B♭m7   E♭6

a long, long time a - go. _____

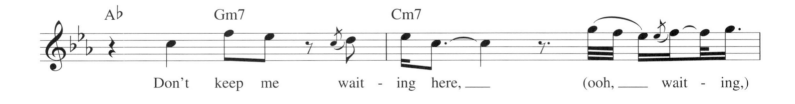

A♭   Gm7   Cm7

Don't keep me wait - ing here, ___ (ooh, ___ wait - ing,)

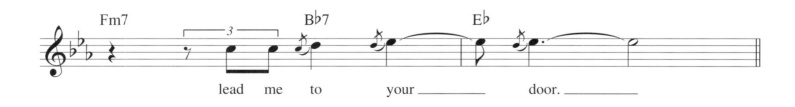

Fm7   3   B♭7   E♭

lead me to your ___ door. _____

Outro

N.C. B♭9sus   E♭

Yeah, yeah, yeah, ___ yeah. ___

Lucy in the Sky with Diamonds

Words and Music by John Lennon and Paul McCartney

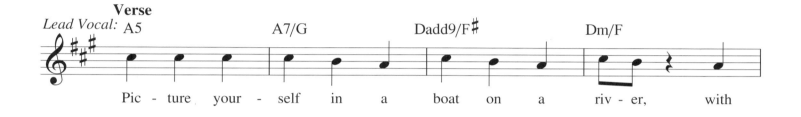

Pic - ture your - self in a boat on a riv - er, with

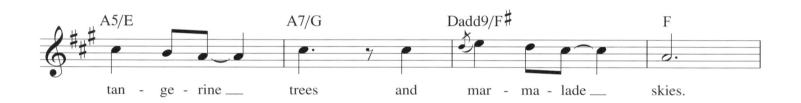

tan - ge - rine ___ trees and mar - ma - lade ___ skies.

Some - bod - y calls ___ you, you an - swer quite ___

slow - ly, a girl with ka - lei - do - scope eyes. ___

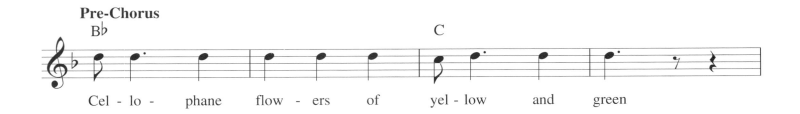

Pre-Chorus

Cel - lo - phane flow - ers of yel - low and green

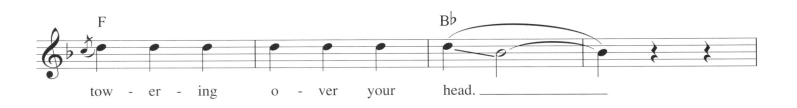

tow - er - ing o - ver your head. _____

Look for the girl _____ with the sun in her

Chorus

eyes, and she's gone. Lu - cy in the sky ___ with

dia - monds. Lu - cy in the sky ___ with dia - monds.

Verse
Tempo I

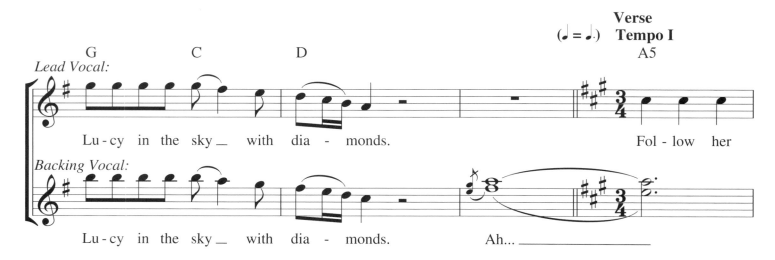

Lead Vocal:

Lu - cy in the sky ___ with dia - monds. Fol - low her

Backing Vocal:

Lu - cy in the sky ___ with dia - monds. Ah... _____

down to a ___ bridge by a foun-tain, where rock-ing horse _

peo-ple eat marsh-mal-low pies. ___ Ev-'ry-one

smiles as you drift past the flow - ers that grow so in-

cred - i - bly high. _____

Pre-Chorus

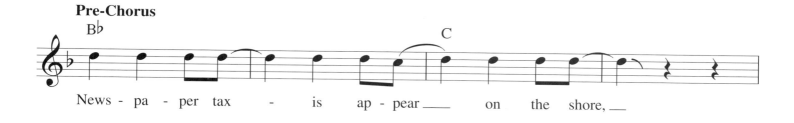

News-pa-per tax - is ap-pear ___ on the shore, ___

wait - ing to take ___ you a - way. _____

Climb in the back ___ with your ___ head in the clouds __ and you're _

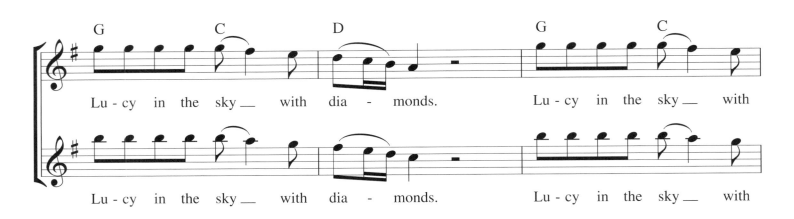

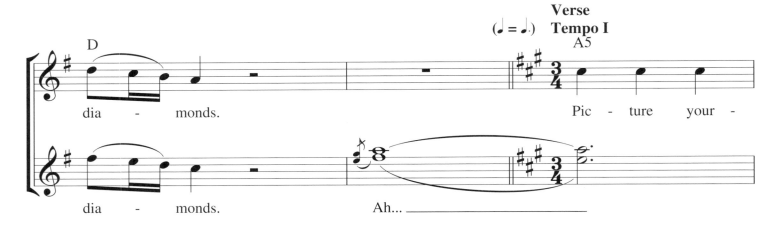

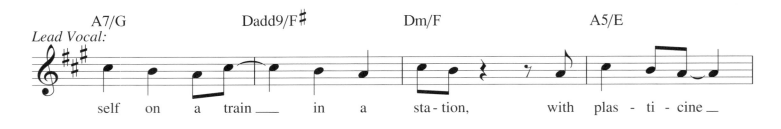

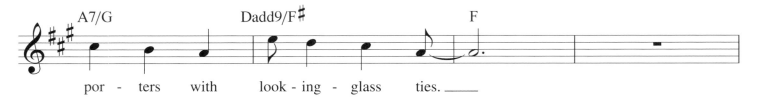

Sud - den - ly, some - one is there at the turn - stile: the

girl with ka - lei - do - scope eyes. _____

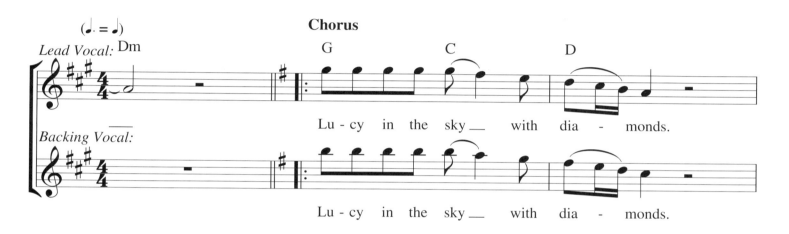

Chorus

Lead Vocal:

Lu - cy in the sky ___ with dia - monds.

Backing Vocal:

Lu - cy in the sky ___ with dia - monds.

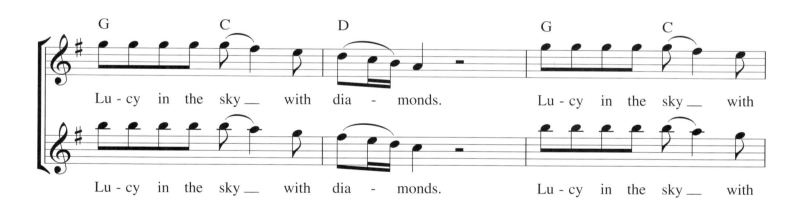

Lu - cy in the sky ___ with dia - monds. Lu - cy in the sky ___ with

Lu - cy in the sky ___ with dia - monds. Lu - cy in the sky ___ with

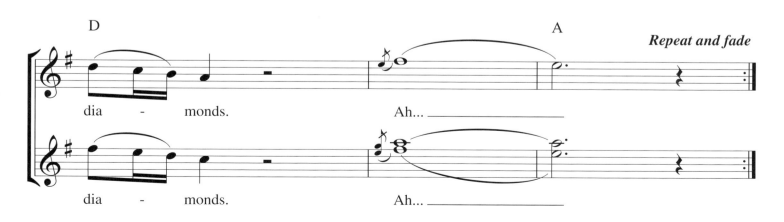

Repeat and fade

dia - monds. Ah... _____

dia - monds. Ah... _____

Norwegian Wood
(This Bird Has Flown)

Words and Music by John Lennon and Paul McCartney

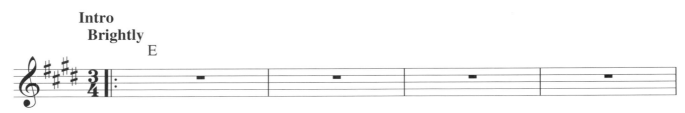

I once had a girl, ____ or should I ____

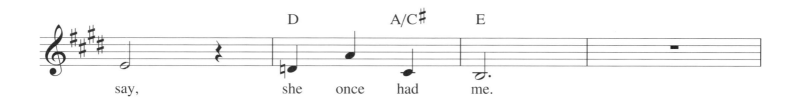

say, she once had me.

She showed me her ___ room. Is - n't it

good? Nor - we - gian wood.

Bridge

Lead Vocal:

She asked me to stay and she told me to

Backing Vocal:

She asked me to stay and she told me to

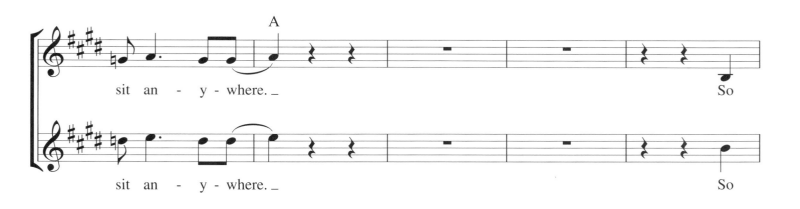

sit an - y - where. So

sit an - y - where. So

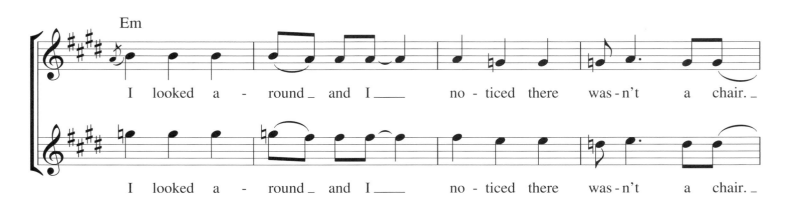

I looked a - round and I no - ticed there was - n't a chair.

I looked a - round and I no - ticed there was - n't a chair.

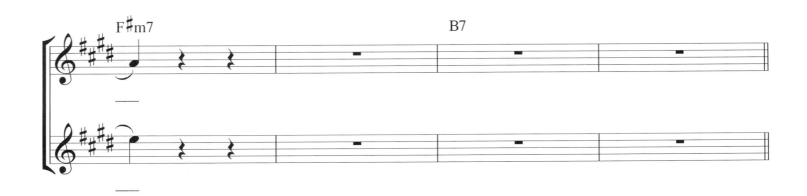

Verse

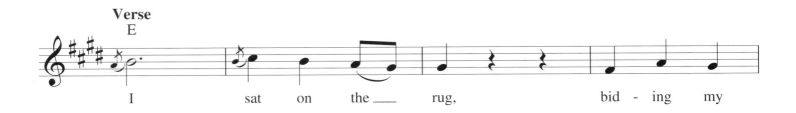

I sat on the ___ rug, biding my

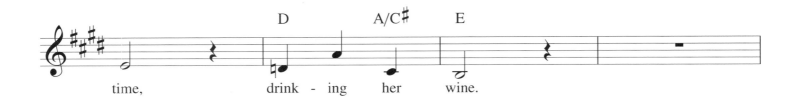

time, drink - ing her wine.

We talked un - til ___ two, and then she

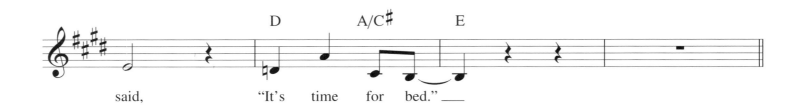

said, "It's time for bed." ___

Interlude

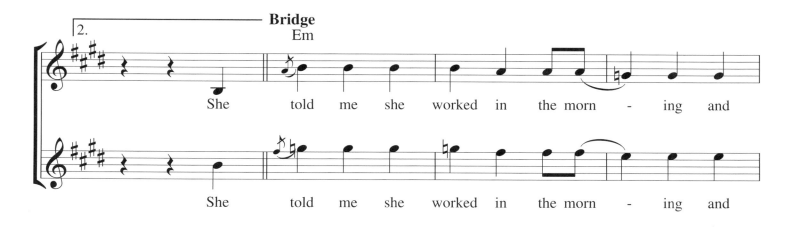

Bridge

She told me she worked in the morn - ing and

She told me she worked in the morn - ing and

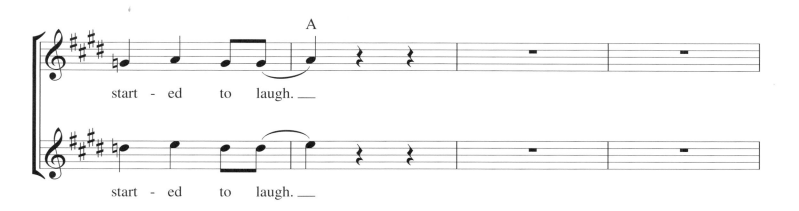

start - ed to laugh. ___

start - ed to laugh. ___

I told her I did - n't, and crawled ___ off to

I told her I did - n't, and crawled ___ off to

sleep in the bath. ___

sleep in the bath. ___

Verse

And when I ___ a - woke, I was a -

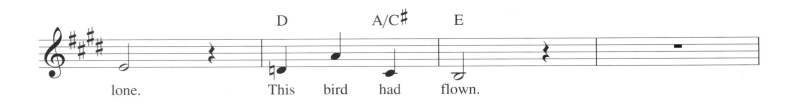

lone. This bird had flown.

So I lit the ___ fire. Is - n't it

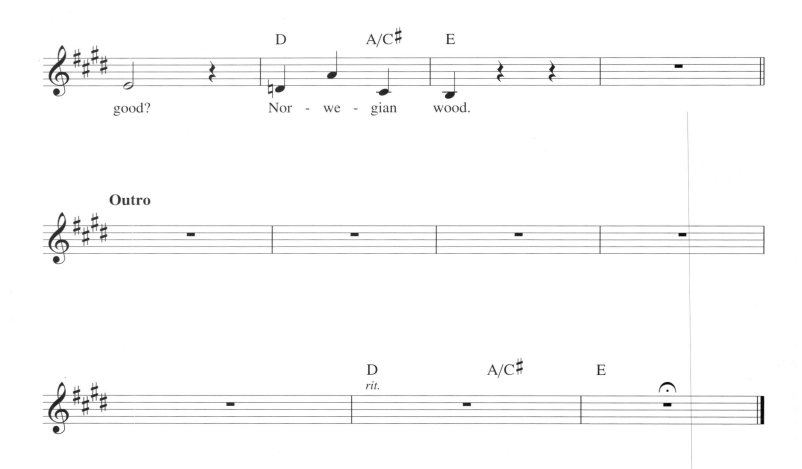

good? Nor - we - gian wood.

Outro